First Questions and Answers about the **City**

DO SKYSCRAPERS TOUCH THE SKY?

TIME
LIFE *for*
Children®

ALEXANDRIA, VIRGINIA

Contents

Do skyscrapers touch the sky?

No, but some of them are so tall they poke through rain clouds. That's because a city is a crowded place where many people live, work, and play. To hold all those people, the buildings have to go way up into the sky. These tall buildings are called skyscrapers.

5

Why is there so much traffic in the city?

Because so many people have so many places to go!
Taxis, cars, and buses carry people through the city.
Delivery vans take food to stores. Cement mixers
and dump trucks bring concrete and sand to make
new buildings. Repair trucks fix the streets. Garbage
trucks pick up trash and haul it away.

Why do traffic lights change colors?

The colors tell drivers when to stop and go. Red means "Stop!" Green means "Go!" Yellow means "Slow down—this light is about to turn red!" Most cities have signs to help you cross the street. When it's safe to cross, the signs show a person walking, or they say "Walk." When the signs show a raised hand or say "Don't walk," you have to wait on the sidewalk.

Don't forget to cross at the corner!

Did you know?
Even when the light is green and the sign says "Walk," be sure to look both ways before you step into the street.

Where are all the people going?

People in a city may be on their way to work or school. They may be coming home from a grocery store or music lessons. Runners, walkers, skaters, and bikers are getting their exercise. Visitors are looking for the famous buildings and places they've read about in books.

Where do people stay when they visit a city?

Visitors usually stay in hotels. A hotel is a building with lots of bedrooms and bathrooms. People pay money to sleep there overnight. The hotel may also have a gift shop, an exercise room, a swimming pool, a restaurant, and a room for playing video games.

Where do city people live?

Most city people live in apartment buildings, which are divided on the inside into groups of rooms called apartments. An apartment may have one room or ten. Some apartment buildings hold just two or three families; others are home to hundreds of people.

Do animals live in the city?

The city is home to many wild animals—squirrels, birds, mice, rabbits, and chipmunks. Bees, ants, and other insects live there, too. Many city animals are household pets. On every street you can see different kinds of dogs being walked by their owners. Cats make good apartment pets because they are so quiet.

Did you know?
Some city animals have special jobs. Horses carry police officers into parks where cars can't go.

Where do children play?

City children go to parks to run and jump and play ball. They go to playgrounds to climb on the jungle gym and swing on the swings. Some cities have ponds where children can sail toy boats, or ice rinks where they can skate. With so many children in the city, there's always someone to play with!

A park is a great place to make new friends!

What's under the street?

Many things that make a city work are under the ground. There's no room for them up above!

Water pipes bring clean water for drinking and washing. Other pipes carry away the dirty water.

Telephone wires
are underground, too.

Wires carry electricity to turn on lights.

What is a subway?

Subways are fast trains that run on tracks through tunnels beneath the streets. The trains carry people from place to place quickly. Usually they move faster than cars on the street. That's because there's no traffic to slow the trains down.

Did you know?
In some cities you need a special coin, called a token, to ride the subway.

How do people know which bus to ride?

On the front of every bus is a sign that says where the bus is going. Each bus follows its own special path, or route, through the city. If the route has a number, that number appears on the front of the bus, too. The bus picks up people and lets them off all along its route.

Let's explore some more!

Did you know?
In the United States, buses carry
more people than planes, trains,
or subways.

What is a museum?

A museum is a place filled with things that people want to see and learn about. Some museums hold beautiful paintings or rocks and jewels. Others show how animals and insects live in nature. History museums teach what life was like many years ago.

Try it!
Pretend you are building
a museum to hold the things
you like best. What would
you put in it?

What happens in a theater?

A theater is a building where people act out stories called plays. People sit in soft chairs to watch the play. When the play is about to begin, the lights go down and the curtain goes up. The actors wear costumes and walk (or run!) around a stage. Sometimes an orchestra plays music in front of the stage.

Why is it so noisy in the city?

It's hard for so many exciting things to happen without making noise! Machines that build and fix things make loud noises. So do the motors and horns of cars and trucks and buses. Everything makes its own special sound: Bicycle bells ding, taxi horns beep, and subway trains rumble.

Try it!
Many different sounds are being made here. How many of them can you make?

What are sirens for?

They warn people to get out of the way—emergency vehicles are coming through! Fire trucks, police cars, and ambulances have to get to the scene of an emergency fast. They sound their sirens so other drivers will pull over and let them by.

How are fires put out in tall buildings?

Firefighters can reach the upper floors of most tall buildings with a ladder on their truck. Two firefighters stand at the top of the ladder and spray water on the fire with a hose. Other firefighters attach hoses to fire hydrants on the ground and spray water on the lower floors.

Did you know?
No ladder is long enough to reach the top of a skyscraper. Firefighters go into the building and turn on special water pumps to put out the fire.

How is a skyscraper built?

First, workers hammer long steel bars into the ground. The bars act like legs to hold the building up. Next, the frame goes up. It looks like a cage and is made of metal bars called girders. Walls and floors are added, then wires and pipes go inside the walls. When the outside is done, the inside is painted and decorated. All that's needed now is people!

Did you know?
A construction crane can lift bars as heavy as 16 elephants.

37

What is a revolving door?

A revolving door is split into three or four pieces, like the pieces of a pie. When you push on the glass, the door revolves, or turns. This takes you in or out of the building. Some buildings need revolving doors because they get so many visitors. A revolving door lets one person go into the building at the same time another comes out.

Did you know?
Some revolving doors have brakes that slow down the doors if they start turning too fast.

39

How does an elevator work?

Steel cables pull the elevator up and down. When people get on the elevator, they push a button marked with the number of the floor they want to visit. The button starts a motor. The motor moves the cables, and the cables lift or lower the elevator to that floor.

41

How do they clean all those windows?

Workers wash them one by one! The window washers stand on a platform that works like an elevator; it is pulled up the side of the building by cables attached to a crane on the roof. The platform holds buckets of water, squeegees, and soap. The window washers wear safety belts while they work.

Did you know?
It takes about two weeks to wash a skyscraper!

43

What can you see from the top of the city?

The whole world—or so it seems! That's because there are no buildings to block the view. You can see terraces and balconies where people grow flowers and plants. You can see rooftop tanks where water is stored. Things on the ground look small. Cars look like tiny toys. Trees look like bushy green flowers. And people look like moving dots.

45

What does the city look like at night?

At night the city glitters with light. Skyscrapers have lights on top to warn planes away. Apartment windows glow like golden blocks. Lights on bridges make bright, shiny chains. The city stays awake all night.

Z-z-z-z.

TIME-LIFE for CHILDREN ®

Managing Editor: Patricia Daniels
Editorial Directors: Jean Burke Crawford, Allan Fallow,
Karin Kinney, Sara Mark
Senior Art Director: Susan K. White
Editorial Coordinator: Marike van der Veen
Editorial Assistant: Mary M. Saxton
Production Manager: Marlene Zack
Senior Copyeditor: Colette Stockum
Production: Celia Beattie
Supervisor of Quality Control: James King
Assistant Supervisor of Quality Control: Miriam Newton
Library: Louise D. Forstall, Anne Heising

Special Contributor: Barbara Klein
Researcher: Fran Kalavritinos
Writer: Jacqueline A. Ball

Designed by: **David Bennett Books Ltd**

Series design: David Bennett
Book design: David Bennett
Art direction: David Bennett
Illustrated by: Peter Kavanagh
**Additional cover
  illustrations by:**   Nick Baxter

First printing. Printed in U.S.A.
Published simultaneously in Canada.

Time Life Inc. is a wholly owned subsidiary of THE TIME INC. BOOK COMPANY.

TIME-LIFE is a trademark of Time Warner Inc. U.S.A.

For subscription information, call 1-800-621-7026.

School and library distribution by Time-Life Education,
P.O. Box 85026, Richmond, VA 23285-5026.

Library of Congress Cataloging-in-Publication Data
Do Skyscrapers touch the sky?: first questions and answers about
the city.
p. cm. (Time-Life library of first questions and answers)
ISBN 0-7835-0886-7 (hardcover). ISBN 0-7835-0887-5 (library)
1. Cities and towns-Miscellanea-Juvenile literature. [1. Cities and towns-Miscellanea. 2. Questions and answers.]
I. Time-Life for Children (Firm) II. Series: Library of first questions and answers.
HT152.D6 1995
307.76-dc20
94-18199

CIP
AC

Consultants

Dr. Lewis P. Lipsitt, an internationally recognized specialist in
childhood development, was the 1990 recipient of the Nicholas Hobbs
Award for science in the service of children. He has served as the science
director for the American Psychological Association and is a professor of
psychology and medical science at Brown University.

Dr. Judith A. Schickedanz, an authority on the education of preschool
children, is an associate professor of early childhood education at the
Boston University School of Education, where she also directs the Early
Childhood Learning Laboratory. Her published work includes *More Than
the ABCs: Early Stages of Reading and Writing Development* as well as
several textbooks and many scholarly papers.